Tick-Tock

poems by

Peggy Schimmelman

Finishing Line Press
Georgetown, Kentucky

Tick-Tock

Copyright © 2019 by Peggy Schimmelman
ISBN 978-1-63534-931-3 First Edition
All rights reserved under International and Pan-American Copyright Conventions. No part of this book may be reproduced in any manner whatsoever without written permission from the publisher, except in the case of brief quotations embodied in critical articles and reviews.

ACKNOWLEDGMENTS

Prior Publication:

Marin Poetry Center Anthology: "Tick-tock"
Sparkle 'n Blink (Quiet Lightning): "The Last Lullaby"
Wild Musette Journal: "A Poem in Three"
Eunoia: "Porch Step Twelve-Bar Blues," "In My Mother's Voice"
Comstock Review: "Nocturne"
Pacific Review: "The Low Road"
Las Positas Anthology: "This Must Be Death," "The Color of Midnight"
Haight-Ashbury Literary Journal: "Carnival Days," "Oops, You Missed It!"

The following poems appeared in *Crazytown*, a Peggy Shimmelman chapbook published by Writing Knight's Press: "The Last Lullaby," "Nocturne" "The Color of Midnight"

I'm grateful for the support of my writing group, Wild Vine Writers, who encourage and inspire me through innovative writing prompts, exposure to wonderful writing, and insightful critiques. Whistlestop Writers, a monthly Livermore writer's gathering hosted by Livermore Poet Laureate Cynthia Patton, provides motivation and inspiration through interaction with other poets and writers. Finally, I want to thank my husband, Paul Schimmelman, who tolerates the highs and lows of my creative cycle and coaxes me through periods of self-doubt and/or self-absorption, for which I am exceedingly grateful.

Publisher: Leah Maines
Editor: Christen Kincaid
Cover Art: Paul Schimmelman
Author Photo: Paul Schimmelman
Cover Design: Leah Huete

Printed in the USA on acid-free paper.
Order online: www.finishinglinepress.com
also available on amazon.com

Author inquiries and mail orders:
Finishing Line Press
P. O. Box 1626
Georgetown, Kentucky 40324
U. S. A.

Table of Contents

Tick-Tock 1
Porch Step Twelve-Bar Blues 2
Carnival Days 3
Four-Minute Shower 4
The Last Lullaby 5
Nocturne 6
The Wilds of Midnight 7
Road Work 8
In My Mother's Voice 9
In the Hurricane's Wake 10
House of Diversion 11
One of Those Nights 12
Sins of Our Fathers (For Mother Earth) 13
Incriminating Evidence 15
Brown-eyed Nightmare 17
Reluctant Muse 18
It's All in Your Mind 19
Like a Worn-out Shoe 20
Rebellion 21
Dead Man's Journey 22
Goodbye Would Have Sufficed 23
Season of Aggrievement (2017) 24
The Color of Midnight (Since You've Been Gone) 25
The Low Road 26
Mojave Moon 28
Why You Must Return Soon (Downbeat) 29
A Poem in Three 30
At St. Vincent de Paul 31
Disarray 33
Oops, You Missed It! 35

Tick-tock

even now
while the meteors fly
on this Leonid night
and the lusty cat yowls
outside your transom

even now
with hope in remission
dreams in the closet
your gypsy soul dances
wild in the night

even now
as her jangling tambourine
demands contrition
for journeys not taken
inspiration wasted

even now
while your past is present
in fragmented swatches
know that your future
is revealing itself
one
        tick-tock
at a time.

Porch Step Twelve-Bar Blues

Some nights the blues just keep on comin'
and all you can do is to strum that guitar
hummin' some twelve-bar three chord tune
about a moonstruck mama
        or a gamblin' man
                or your damn empty wallet
and you wail it to the stars 'cause so far
nobody else seems to want to listen.

So you throw in a verse about God's indifference
not paying attention, not fixing the holes
in your low-down, bottomed-out, not-fair luck.
You're not asking much
        a little cash above rent money
                lovin' in the midnight
a low-light, open mic blues jam
where people let you play your music.

Now thunder's rollin' in like a drunked-up drummer
heavy on the downbeat
        draggin' on the backbeat
                jackin' up the time
          messin' with your shuffle.
But you can't quit now
got to write 'em where you find 'em
rope 'em in before they run

'cause your muse is in the porch swing
with one eye on the highway.
Why, tomorrow that girl might hit the road thumbin'
but tonight
those blues just keep on comin'.

Carnival Days

This tilt-a-whirl planet spins and pivots
rattles my spirit, dizzies my soul.
Those sudden swerves they slip and slide me
How can one expect, at the end of the day
to walk a straight line or think clearly?

My friend rides the carousel, dreamy-eyed
as around she goes in predictable circles
ups and downs gentle, the music merry
nostalgic, hypnotic, and chosen to give her
nothing she won't want to hear.

Now come the screams, glee swirled with fear
from the roller coaster
        zipping
                dipping:

"Wahoo!" shouts one.
"Let me off!" wails another.
As into the Fun House I stumble again
she tightens her grip on the unicorn's mane
and sways to the sweet calliope.

Four-Minute Shower

Was it thunder I heard just now
below the soothing white noise of the shower?
Soap and scrub, shampoo and rinse
all hurried along by the clock
and that intermittent ominous rumble.
But alas, no rain in the forecast
as the drought drags on into springtime
our earth so thirsty I'm swimming in guilt
over watering my plants or indulging myself
in more than a four-minute shower.

Perhaps it's my new neighbor's Harley
revving up with a sinister roar—
the same one that almost ran over me
as I jogged past his driveway this morning
after which I was asked: was I friggin' deaf
did I not hear the bike
we could've both been killed
or the Harley totaled and then by god
he would have sued my ass
to hell and back, believe it.

Flashback: my hammering heart
I stammer I'm sorry
his smirking wife smokes in the doorway
red-eyed devil-dog snarls
and now, in defiance of the four-minute bell
I'm swept downstream
by a deluge of stinging comebacks
sarcastic putdowns
while the suds seek the drain
along with some spatters of fury
and there it is again, that rumbling.

It might be the local high school band
marching on the field at half-time
or the five o'clock train running early
but still, though the sky is as spotless
as my new neighbor's Harley
I could almost have sworn
I heard thunder.

The Last Lullaby

Selam and Adonay, hush now and sleep.
Boat men don't like it when little ones weep.
Ahead, Europe waits to shelter and feed us—
to welcome us. Children, now listen to me:

nightmares can't reach you out here on the sea.
Aziz and Rahwa, please hush now and sleep.
Visions of villages, ravaged and charred
will fade like ghosts, left to die on the water.

Eritrea, Gambia, Nigeria, Ghana
the souls of your slaughtered are singing to me.
Semirah and Hanna, hush now and sleep.
All boats list and lurch, there is nothing to fear:

with God watching over, rescue is near.
As we slip from the edge, slide into the deep,
Semirah, Hanna, Rahwa, Aziz,
Selam and Adonay, hush now and sleep.

Nocturne

Something not quite right
in this restless
wide awake night
stars slipping out
of cozy constellations
like teenage daughters
through bedroom windows
embracing boyfriends
beneath a leering
lopsided moon
while the humid breeze scolds
and the mockingbirds fret
like despairing mothers
whose fragile nests
have shifted off-kilter
        tipped
and started
to tumble
through
time.

The Wilds of Midnight

Here I go
on the run again, lost
in the wilds of midnight
wondering
if both hands are needed
to measure years remaining
or would the fingers
of one hand suffice?
Maybe
I could also count on a toe
or three or five.

Alive
is not taken for granted here
in this haunted jungle
where time is both stalker
and prey
circling itself
closing in on me
as I shudder under
the heat of its breath
knowing
how this hunt must end.
Still

I will count
my digits and wait—
make my escape
under cover of daybreak.
Won't life
(suspecting I'm done for)
be surprised
when I spring from my quilts
and make yet another
brave and defiant
run for it?

Road Work

Rules learned at fifteen
have blurred with time.
Like how much space
should I allow in between
and when is a U-turn advisable?
Could a red light mean Go
if signals get switched?
Is Yield now a sign of weakness?

It's hard to misinterpret
        Road Work Ahead:
slow the heck down
shut off the engine
or waste my fuel as I mutter, curse, fret
thrum my fingers on the wheel.
No new messages, calls, or texts.
Check, recheck, and wait.

I remind myself that Men at Work
if they do their job right
can repair damage wrought
by excess traffic and heavy loads
which should result in fewer potholes
right-of-ways clearly defined
and lanes distinctly divided.

But in my experience
        Highway Improvement
is an ongoing process that gobbles up time
is taxing, vexing
raises blood pressure and most perplexing
doesn't always guarantee
a less bumpy ride in the future.

In My Mother's Voice

I sit by her tomb as she chastises me
in a boneyard strewn
with hillbilly ancestors
neighbors and friends
all bearing witness to memories and regrets
enshrouding me in silent rebuke
as she rather unkindly reminds me
how I fled the Ozarks at seventeen
got above my raising
brought home my uppity up-north accent
college learning
scoffed at my kinfolks' ain'ts and cain'ts
double negatives
disregard for subject-verb agreement.

But that's past, she says
and other than that
you was a pretty good daughter
and I been right sorry
I couldn't help none
when you had them troubles.
I went and passed too young.
I done let you down.
Forgive me.

On her grave I left a dime store bouquet
conciliatory tears
and some words I knew would please her:
 "You never done no such a thing," I said.
You was there the whole time.
 I seen you."

In the Hurricane's Wake

In retrospect, warnings were everywhere.
On your phone, your computer
from the lips of friends
and most chilling:
you whispered them in your sleep.

First came that prickling sensation:
an ill breeze rising.
But even as windowpanes shuddered
against swirling winds and
thunderous rain
it still seemed possible to stand my ground.
I would pray, keep the faith
ride it out.

As you made your escape
the ocean's roar ripped through my denial
shattered windows, splintered doorways
sent me fleeing up-up-up
and now here I am

that pathetic creature you see on the rooftop
awaiting rescue
watching my treasures float downstream
while observers, even you
must wonder:
was she blind
or deaf
or mentally challenged?
Otherwise, how in God's name
did she manage to not see this coming?

House of Diversion

One arrow points left, another right
both promise surprises and sure enough
        the floor undulates
                we bounce off the walls
      stumble along
avoiding the mirrors
      dismayed by reflections of
bewildered
      dizzy
             misshapen creatures
who can't find the door at the end of the maze
      which is marked with arrows
      that point both ways
and all signs read: Caution
      Diversion Alert
          Turn right for the truth
but when we do, what do you know?
There's another arrow pointing us left.

We won't despair, there's an end to this madness
though it seems we've been trapped for eons
      while the hands on the clock spin
          wildly and
                manic cuckoos
      spring forth at random
with insults that feel like warnings.
But that's only a fake impression
more fun house shenanigans, surely.

If we scream loud enough, rescue will come
but how will we know whom to trust?
This trickery
      contortion
            disorientation
has left us jaded
      suspicious
and we can only pray that
overexposure to toxic smoke
hasn't forever distorted our vision.

One of Those Nights

Some midnights are darker than others
that vast blue blackness
having nothing to do
with phases of the moon or bad weather

and the wind doesn't carry those demons
who scratch at your soul
or the fretful undead
who moan their regrets at your window.

It's useless to pray for sleep, that valley
where memories compete
to expose themselves
in fragmented "Why?"-rated movies.

Oh why can't they listen to reason
give haunting a rest
come back with the morning
negotiations of sorts, over coffee?

You would welcome that ghoulish agenda
grievances vented
in your safe sunlit kitchen
if only they'd sleep through your midnight.

But your demons trust only the darkness.
It's closer to home
and always delivers
your distraught, undivided attention.

Sins of Our Fathers (For Mother Earth)

Will you hold us, Mother?
Tell us a story with a happy ending?
Sing us a lullaby, rock us to sleep
that we may not dream
of our sisters and brothers
murdering, maiming
with bombs and guns: fratricide
in the name of our fathers.

Your children at war
hell bent on preserving the lineage
striving to spread the patriarchal seed
in numbers enough to conquer, control
not only mankind but you,
mother of us all.

Do you despair, mother
for the sins of your children
as we deplete your air, poison your water
distract ourselves with trivialities
while your glaciers melt
your oceans swell, your unique creations
species after species, cease to be?

Do you ever cry out to those gods
our fathers
"Enough! No more!
as from your womb we continue to stream
in numbers too many to feed?

Whom do you blame?
Is it us, your children?
Or the blood of our fathers, those gods
who planted the seeds of greed, lust, hatred
and left us alone
to interpret their teachings as best we can
which so far is not good enough.

Will you hold us, mother?
Won't you tell us a story with a happy ending

if we run to your arms
press our ears to your heart
and listen?

Incriminating Evidence

I know it looks bad:
dust bunnies reproducing beneath the bed
laundry erupting from hampers
dishes migrating from sink to countertops
and everywhere you look
a stack of books
some poetry I've been meaning to get to
a pile of New Yorkers on the bedside table
sneering at my lack of attention.

What's going on here?
(you want to ask, but are too polite)
I feel your alarm, though unspoken
as I brush cat hairs from the sofa
where we sit to converse over coffee.

An apology would not be honest.
Life feels so fleeting, my friend.
Christmases coming so close together
I never get around to taking down lights
or returning bells to the shed.

This and my long-time aversion to cleaning
have led to a new routine.
I choose not to notice, these days
that inner voice that suggests I'm lazy
and to ignore the damning evidence
that is piling up all around me.

Thing are not as they seem.
I'm not a slothful, slovenly woman
it's just that I'm so much happier now
with all these free hours to write and submit
keep track of rejections
sharing successes, frustrations, failures
as you've no doubt noticed on Facebook.

Yes, I know it looks bad
but I'm healthy, I promise.
Please try to accept my revised priorities

as has my husband
who, as you may have surmised
is also no fan of housework.

Brown-eyed Nightmare

From beneath my bed crept pure, magnificent evil
        that smirk
        that swagger
        that scent of wild nights past.
Starlit skin, torture in his eyes.
Unmerciful.

You're a dream now, I told him. Powerless
        those teeth
        those shoulders
        those wicked hips.
He faded, I awoke.
Safe, in the unreachable present.

But in retreat, his parting shot—
        that curve of his lips
        that tease in his voice
        that fire in his touch—
ripped open my heart, spilling jagged regrets
searing what ifs
        and lonely
all over my pillow.

Reluctant Muse

She's late again and when she arrives
I'm demoralized by her doubts and derision:
too old, she says, creativity spent
too scattered, too shallow
a waste of her time.

But still, she tries: rolling her eyes at my
misunderstanding, erratic rearranging
of her metaphoric images and near perfect rhymes.
Hopeless, she says, a waste of her time
untalented, distracted, over-caffeinated, anxious
too old, uninspired, creativity spent.

Somehow it happens: a line or a phrase
another, then another
time and place disappear
as I remake her vision into my own.

Then more often than not
she dismisses my effort
taking her leave with no promise to return:
trivial, vapid, overwrought, derivative
hopeless, she says, creativity spent
untalented, scattered
shallow, uninspired
too old, she says.
A waste of her time.

It's All in Your Mind

Sometimes like crazy I miss those days.
Lazy Sunday mornings on a screened-in porch
coffee and bagels
headlines and comics
chanting along with classic Stones:
"Shattered" in those days
was only a song.

I followed you onto the train last night.
Heard you sigh as you took her call.
Saw you wince at her shrill accusations.
Laughed as you told her:
It's all in your mind.

I love you, you said. It's all in your mind.
There is no woman who drives by the house
slowly, too slowly, day after day.
That face in the window:
it's all in your mind.

The dozen dead roses tossed onto the porch
was a prank, nothing more
that bomb threat at work was random
the Death card a psychic misreading.
Trust me, you said. It's all in your mind.

I smiled to remember those Sundays we had
when you were still you and I was still I
and we were still us on a screened-in porch
before you first spoke those same words to me:
I love you, you said. It's all in your mind.

I miss those days, sometimes like crazy.

Like a Worn-out Shoe

High-heels or flats
huaraches or sneakers
marching dancing
skipping shuffling
working in synch
first one then the other
propelling us forward
a step at a time
so that we're always
as we move through life
unconsciously waiting
for one shoe
or the other
to drop.

At day's end we slip them off:
right then the left
lining them up
if they're still new enough
side by side on the shoe rack.
If they've seen better days
we give them a toss
to the back of the closet—

and they languish there
like a jealous lover
scuffed and run-down
a hole in his soul
having witnessed betrayal
waiting for the sound
of stilettos on the stairs
dreading that moment
when the door swings open
and the other shoe
—we need to talk—
will inevitably
irreversibly
drop.

Rebellion

My hips have gone pirate
provoking unrest
among thighs, discs, spine
their anarchic agenda
forcing upon me
the unacceptable
acceptance of aging—
that inevitable limp
off the plank.

Their selfish revolt
has foiled my efforts
to unify, strengthen
mind, heart and lungs—
those more loyal factions
who understand:
when Neptune beckons
and the ship's going down
there's all the more reason
to dance.

Dead Man's Journey

Our scientists knew, as the test bomb flared
in the Jornado del Muerto desert
you can't whistle back the hounds of Hell.
This world is not ours for the keeping.

You cannot unwhisper such secrets.
A radioactive virus on a siren's song
greedy, indiscriminate, consuming the souls
of physicists, generals, and tyrants.

Uranus, Pluto, please guide us.
Might sanity prevail
on this war-possessed earth, or
shall we ready ourselves for the reaping?

Goodbye Would Have Sufficed

A poor soul; left her heart in Peet's this morning.
It slid to the floor along with her phone
as she sat mesmerized by the man's guilty eyes
and the cascade of justification he spewed
while searching for the single word
that would have summed it up succinctly.

She stuffed crumpled tissues into her purse
struggled into her parka and waited, stunned
until he, relieved and so ready to go
took her elbow and with gentle impatience
nudged her toward the exit.

I retrieved the phone
and followed them out to return it.
Her heart I left lying on the coffee house floor
bruised and in shock.
She didn't ask after it so perhaps she knows
though she'll miss it dearly
that hearts, unlike phones
may take months to recharge
and must find their own way back home.

Season of Aggrievement (2017)

Mother was a witch all summer.
Helpless, we fled for shelter
as she roiled like a hurricane
an earthquake
a ravenous forest fire.
Our prayers bounced off
the ears of our fathers
as she lashed out
ferocious and spiteful
showing us who holds the power.

Now, as she simmers in silence
might we please dispense
with the name-calling
hair-pulling
face-scratching
familial tit-for-tat
while we pause to consider
our mother's complaints
because sooner or later
she'll lose it again—

and when she finally gets enough
of our sass and neglect
oh brother you betcha
there's gonna be
worse hell to pay.

The Color of Midnight (Since You've Been Gone)

When the night comes down
around this house
it's not in shades of blue-black-gray
but in billowing waves
       of blood-red fury
               envy, venom-green
         confusion, foggy-purple
                 blinding-yellow anxiety
and on the worst nights:
       orange, the color of madness—

—when the night comes down
this way:
       relentless, washing away sleep
there's nothing to do but abandon bed
       seek higher ground
             stumble to the sofa
go channel surfing in a sea of inanity:
     late-night chatter
         infomercials
                Seinfeld repeats
         Bacall and Bogie's
     black and white banter
clinging to sanity, swimming through
purple-green-yellow-red- midnight
                    pushing
        back
   the orange
praying for a colorless dawn.

The Low Road

You didn't take the high road
as your mother advised.
From where you stood
it might just as well
have been Kilimanjaro—
rocky, winding, impossibly steep.
Never mind her promise
that at journey's end
having chosen that path
you'd be stronger and wiser
dignity and pride intact.

If only you'd listened
the worst would be over
his cheating a memory
the healing begun.
If only.

Instead:
heart singed by betrayal
you gave them hell
from midnight to dawn
begging him
haranguing her
by phone, by text
by social media
smearing your heartbreak
like angry graffiti
across the startled wall
of the world.

And now you're choking
on the bitter remorse
that comes from succumbing
to temptations found
on the bottom-most stretch
of the low road—
the sweetest of which
was sharing the link
to the damning video

of their naked betrayal
with four hundred thirty-six
Facebook friends
and too many followers
on Twitter.

LOL, right?

Mojave Moon

I shudder at the thought of a coffin
buried deep beneath a tombstone etched
with my essential earthly achievements:
born, died, loving wife and mother.
A teacher and little-known writer.

How dreary to wait in a graveyard
for karmic reassignment
or the call of the seventh trumpet
surrounded by bones
and worm-chewed flesh
a newcomer to starlit soirees
hosted by restless apparitions
of departed neighbors and friends.
Imagine the boredom as nights on end
they debate God's intentions
mull over memories
bemoan their sins and regrets.

No, release my soul to the desert.
Let me soar like an angel enchanted
by that ancient Mojave moon.
I'll commune with coyotes
jack rabbits, geckos
iguanas and Joshua trees.
 I'll sway to the drumbeat
of Shoshone shamans
dance with the spirits
of Serranos, Cahuillas
Gram Parsons and
moon drunk peyote-stoned hippies.

It's not that I'm itching to ditch this town
but we cross only once
that mysterious, inevitable threshold.
If I must take death's arm,
why not let it lead me
to exotic other worlds
where I can speak a new tongue
sing unfamiliar songs and
meet some interesting new people?

Why You Must Return Soon (Downbeat)

This morning I slid from the bed's other side
unblocked by your usual stabilizing presence.
No warm slippers met my feet
just an icy wooden floor to send me skittering
shivering, into the kitchen
where I cancelled work
ate brownies for breakfast
then conquered the crossword
with words I invented
to fill all the white empty spaces.

Boredom invaded as time ticked on.
I might have read, run the vacuum
instead, distracted
I attacked my drum set, unrestrained
by the thought of you wincing
out there in the hallway
no one to remind me
to think of the neighbors
to tell me I'm rushing
or dragging
and maybe my snare needs a tuning.

If you don't return soon
I might lose it completely
plug my earbuds into my iPhone
with no one around to be baffled
or annoyed
as I dance room to room in my socks
shaking off the blues
singing off-key to country rock oldies
and clapping
on the one and the three.

A Poem in Three

Make me your love song
in three-quarter time
conjure me, count me in
one-two-three-*one*-two-three
whisper me whistle me
dance me romance me
woo me infuse me
with rhythm and rhyme.

I'm a Viennese ballroom
a Tennessee dive
I'm denim and crinoline
sawdust and silver
seduce me, unloose me
unwrap me undo me
inhale me consume me
I'm whiskey I'm wine.

I'll Waltz Across Texas
I'm Norwegian Wood
I'm Strauss and Chopin
Jolie Blon, Clementine
so wrangle untangle me
Mr. Bojangle me
I'm Amazing Grace
Sweet Betsy from Pike.

I'm Scarborough Fair
on a Moon River night
Piano man stun me
come fiddle-strum-drum me
croon me retune me
twirl and unfurl me
then swing me and sing me
in three-quarter time.

At St. Vincent de Paul

In the drive-thru donation drop-off
he asks what's in the bag. I tell him:
this chartreuse sweater with tags still on
these size eight jeans for which I've lost hope
six pairs of heart-shaped earrings
a stack of cd's and old videos.

I'll accept those, he says.
Donations are down
so whatever you've got, I'll take it:
even that chair with the shredded upholstery
much loved, I can see, by your cat
that scratching post that looks like new
vomit-stained throw rug, used litter box
mouse-on-a-string, dented lampshade.

Anything? Could you use, perhaps
some worn-out scraps from my memory chest
which is overflowing, no room for new data
such as the name of that Starbuck's barista
or the must-see TV show
my friend recommended this morning?

Let's start with some stale recollections:
ancient ill-chosen romances
snippets of shame
cringe-inducing flashbacks
buckets of guilt
a box of chagrin.

Will you take outworn aspirations
and fantasies frayed at the edges?
Oprah's Book Club, best-selling novel
dreams I keep thinking I've discarded
until they tumble again from the closet.

I accept his thanks and the blank receipt.
Then another memory, raw and recent
hisses, springs with dagger-sharp claws

when he points to your name on the pillow.
Have a nice day, ma'am.
Sure hope things improve.
And I'm sorry, by the way
about Lucy.

Disarray

I just now tripped on a memory
hidden among the clutter
of alliterative phrases
unattached iambs scattered about
like stray socks and underwear
dropped here, tossed there
having never found their way
to the growing laundry pile
in the corner.

For years, it slept undisturbed
among drawers overflowing
with undeveloped metaphors
closet floor littered with
abandoned fragments
of elusive inspiration—
so hard to put together
a presentable, submittable
ensemble.

Rediscovered, it withdraws
like a feral cat, claws and hisses
recoils, burrows deep
into its cobwebby corner
filthy, neglected and
possibly rabid.
Begging to be left alone.

Through the night it growls
whimpers, cries, threatens
until my muse arrives
and together we coax
that pathetic wild creature
into a six-sided
transparent box.

Now it sits on my desk
among pencils, post-its
cups of stale coffee

where it squalls and shrieks
while I rattle the cage
and clench my teeth
as I transcribe its yowls
of anguish.

Oops, You Missed It!

Not now, you say.
It's cold and you're spent
as the wolf moon returns
to spill down its magic
on rovers and lovers
and muse-seeking poets.
We shall have, you promise
so many moons more
to soothe our senses
thrill our spirits
with quaint superstitions
and romantic whims.

But now
as the final moon beckons?
Will you deny, at the end
that stooped, withered creature
who springs from your mirror
frantic
demanding her parka and cane?

In her soul she suspects
the moon never weeps
for the transient shadows below:
Earth's fragile creations
who dance for a time
then dissolve with their dreams
into nothing.

Still, she would bathe
in its splendor.
Will you walk with her down
to the vineyard tonight
as she offers her tribute
of ecstasy, despair
gratitude and fear
regret for not coming sooner—

all balled up together
and hurled at the sky
in one final
primal howl
at the wolf moon?

Peggy Schimmelman is a San Francisco Bay Area writer. Her work includes the poetry chapbook *Crazytown* (Writing Knights Press), the novella *One Day You're a Diamond* (Novella-T) and the novel *Whippoorwills*. She is co-author of *Long Stories Short*, by Wild Vine Writers. Her poetry, memoirs, and short fiction have appeared in *North American Review, Sparkle 'n Blink, WinningWriters.com, NovellaT, the Aleola Journal of Poetry and Art, Pacific Review, Comstock Review, Wild Musette, 100wordstories.org* and others.

Peggy is a regular participant in local poetry events in the Bay Area. Her other interests include painting, reading, and playing percussion for two volunteer musical groups, Sally's Pub and Heart Strings, both of which are dedicated to entertaining veterans, the elderly, children and others in need of uplifting. She is also a crossword and acrostic puzzle enthusiast and creator.

Current projects include a collection of memoir and creative non-fiction with her writing group, Wild Vine Writers.

www.ingramcontent.com/pod-product-compliance
Lightning Source LLC
LaVergne TN
LVHW052258070426
835507LV00036B/3380